"I have known Caroline ... her healing skills a valuable ... rapy. Her clients always feel he ... aling sessions.

Caroline is also a talented communicator, teacher and organizer, getting involved in both lectures and seminars to local GPs at our Post Graduate medical centre here in Canterbury."

— Dr Peter Biggs MD, General Practitioner, Canterbury, England

"What a wonderful book, full of common sense, humour and written from the heart in a practical way. A great introduction to healing."

—Matthew Manning, author of *One Foot in the Stars: The Story of the World's Most Extraordinary Healer*

"Reading Caroline Lathams's book *The Heart of Healing Body Mind and Spirit* is like sitting down for a cup of tea, nestled into a cozy chair while a wise and wonderful great aunt shares her depth of wisdom. This book flows straight from Caroline's heart as a remarkable conversation that can allow you to get to the essense of truly what it is to be a healer. Anyone who wants to learn how to heal or wants to deepen their healing skills can grow from reading this wonderful book."

—Denise Linn, author of *Sacred Space: Clearing and Enhancing the Energy of Your Home*

The author will donate 10% of all her profits from the sale of
this book to Canterbury Tibet Link

The Heart

of

Healing

Body Mind

and

Spirit

Caroline Latham

FINDHORN
Press

© Caroline Latham 2000

First published by Findhorn Press in 2000

ISBN 1 899171 28 2

British Library Cataloguing-in-Publication Data.
A catalogue record for this book is available from the British Library.

Library of Congress Card Number: 99-67787

Layout by Pam Bochel
Illustrations by Jerry Seltzer
Front cover design by Dale Vermeer
Picture of the author by Russell Burden

Printed and bound by J. W. Arrowsmith, Bristol, UK

Published by
Findhorn Press

The Park, Findhorn
Forres IV36 3TY
Scotland
Tel 01309 690582
Fax 01309 690036

P.O. Box 13939
Tallahassee
Florida 32317-3939, USA
Tel 850 893 2920
Fax 850 893 3442

e-mail info@findhornpress.com
findhornpress.com

Contents

Contents

Acknowledgements

For Jigme Khyentse Rinpoche and to all my teachers, named and unnamed, who have led me along the way: The good in this book comes from you, the bad from me. Thank you. It is your copyright.

To my husband and children: for their patience, encouragement, support and love in the face of the everyday me. May I learn to put the contents of this book into action more. Thank you. Thank you especially to Oliver, who listened as I read out the chapters.

To Thierry and Karin for taking me on board. Thank you.

Chapter One
Where to Start

The phone rings frequently. I am asked if I'm running a healing workshop, or "What do I think about the NFSH" (that's the National Federation of Spiritual Healers), or "Is Reiki the same as healing?" or the caller will say, "I know I can heal but where do I start?"

There is one simple answer to that: *start where you are.*

When I'm at some boring drinks party (especially the formal type), and the peremptory question comes up, "And what do you do?" and I reply, "I'm a healer", there are always two types of response. Either the person coughs nervously before talking about the football score and running off to get another drink, or the other type of person screeches merrily, "Wow, gee, that's fantastic, and were you born with 'It', or how did you learn 'It', and how many people have you cured with 'It'?" People are either frightened or fascinated. But I want to know what they think 'It' is?

Before you spend a penny on courses or fill in forms or join this group or other, sit down and consider this. However lacking in self-confidence you may feel, all that you need for healing is within you. Each and everyone of us is at root pure light and energy. To quote Deepak Chopra[1] "If you could see your body as it really is, you'd see a huge void with a few scattered dots and spots and some random electrical discharges".... Einstein of course would quote: $E=Mc^2$. I'll have to leave that to the physicists to explain. What matters to you now is that nobody and absolutely no course is going to 'give' you

[1] Deepak Chopra, *Perfect Weight*

what is already deep within you. Every mother is a natural healer when they hold their child's grazed finger and go, "Dear, dear." Every adult is a healer when they show real compassion for someone's troubles. My own father, who for over forty years has been a GP (in England, your local doctor), always says the most important quality in healing is listening. Anyone who listens is a healer. There is a special quality to listening. Everyone who wants to help has got that magic ingredient, the 'It'. Nobody can give you 'It'. All you can do is develop what's already inside you. And even those have the 'It' who do not know they've got 'It'.

In the Buddhist tradition there is the formal ceremony of 'taking refuge'. Those who go through the ceremony are taking refuge in that so-called 'It': that very thing, when you realise that you have that soft spot within you, that sensitive part, that tender 'It', that potential to help.

Many seekers go off to see the teachers in the hope that they will give them that 'It'. There was one Eastern master who used to say: "I can pretend to give it to you if you would like..." So perhaps the start is to take refuge within yourself right now and realise that you have the potential to help. You don't want pain and you don't want anybody else to have pain.

Any course which helps you do that and gives you your own guidelines would be a good course, but you don't need to expend a huge sum of money on buying something you can't buy. Perhaps the cheapest way of all to develop your potential would be reading this book; I do hope so! I've always been an advocate of the cheap and cheerful (perhaps my Scottish ancestry...) and of the corny but true dictum, 'All the best things in life are free'.

So to start with, decide what is motivating you. Matthew Manning, one of the world's leading healers, expresses this very well: "Do you want to heal because you need love, or because you've got love to give?" If your answer is the latter, please continue. If your answer is the former, please continue too, but realise that you will need to clarify your intention. Perhaps, for you, healing will begin more as a journey within.

Intention and motivation are all. Rupert Sheldrake, the well-known biologist, once explained it this way: if you have a dog and leave it at home while you go on vacation to, say, Italy, then the moment you stand up and decide "I'm going to go home now," that's the precise moment when the dog peering out your window back at home goes "mmmm, mmmm." That's how powerful your intentions are. So before you even think of laying your hands on someone, check your motivation. If you intend to help and have the motivation to help, then that thought is very powerful in its own right. I've known people with all sorts of problems who just stick their hands out to help while still continuing their negative train of thought. I am convinced the recipient will feel that negativity. Make the other person more important than yourself.

Wouldn't the world be such a very special place if we stopped worrying? You know the type of thing. You ring your mother up to tell her you haven't got the job you applied for, but you're hoping you might get the next one. Your mother begins to carry on: "Oh dear, darling, how dreadful. In my day it was so much easier. Nowadays nobody's job is safe. Even if you get the job, you may lose it the next day. Look at Danny. Remember him? So sad, so tragic. Don't know how he manages to feed them all. Lucky you're still single. But then I suppose they think you might go off and have babies. Don't believe a word about equal opportunities! Until the men have the babies, women will be stigmatised. Oh, aah. And so much competition. Maybe it's my fault. Maybe helping you to get to the best university and your getting that first, that wasn't helpful after all. Maybe you should have been a cleaner like me."

And on and on. By the time you've put down the phone you're fed up to the back teeth and in complete despair. Your confidence is so low you don't even want to go for the next job interview.

But it doesn't stop there. Your mother then carries on and on to everyone she meets about how tragic your life is, and what can she do, and how bad the world is today. And the people she talks to concur and encourage her with more doom and gloom stories.

Do you see a bit of you in that? We seem to love concentrating on the negative, exaggerating it, spreading it and gossiping about it. And the more we do that, the more real it becomes.

I've never been to a workshop where someone hasn't asked: "Do you think the end of the world is coming soon? Don't you think that that prophet got it right and we're all going to blow up in 2008?" Some teachers reply, "I don't understand." I interpret that perhaps as meaning that their vision is so pure they cannot understand how we could have such a negative view. When the same question was put to Denise Linn, she retorted: "Stop thinking it, or you'll start creating it," or some such words. I think it was Deepak Chopra who once turned to the audience at a book launch in England and said, "The only thing wrong with this country is your lack of self-confidence."

What starts off as one person's thought can easily escalate. So it is really very important to watch your thoughts and check where you're going with them. If I can so easily parody the negative thoughts, what would it be like if we enhanced the positive?

Re-picture the scene with your mother. "Mother, I didn't get that job, but I'm going for another interview next week."

"Never mind darling. I really believe the right job will come to you. Just keep trying. If you didn't get that job, you weren't meant to. You didn't quite fit into their sausage machine. Didn't you say this other job was better anyway? I believe in you. I know you can do it. Everyone's got his or her place in this world. It will come when it's meant. I hold that intention deep in my heart, dear, that you'll get the perfect job for you at the perfect moment, and I'll tell my friends to keep on wishing it for you." She then goes off and sees her friends and, true to her word, requests that they hold the vision of her daughter being successful in her next interview.

Why is it I can feel some of you wanting to throw up because what I've just written is so sweet and saccharine? Isn't it strange that we resist love? We can't take it. Isn't that the real problem?

I recently had the extreme good fortune of being with some 5000 people to see His Holiness the Dalai Lama at the Albert Hall in

London. There was a moment for questions and answers and someone (what good fortune for that someone) asked if His Holiness would lead five minutes of meditation for world peace. HH asked the audience if this was what we really wanted, and I am glad to say there was an encouraging roar. So His Holiness agreed. He simply dropped his head, sitting in front of us all on the stage and sat. For five minutes. You could have heard a pin drop in those moments. Such precious moments. I wish I were an enlightened 'fly on the wall' so I could see what effect that had and is still having on world peace. May my present mention of it spread it further. May it rebound and rebound to transform the negativity.

So that's what we're talking about. If you start with yourself and check your motivation, and you make a powerful, strong and positive intention, perhaps you don't even need to lay your hands on that other person. You are healing already. And if you keep on doing it, you are continuously healing. And if we all do it??... All the time. Forget the sixties. Then they talked about it. Long live the nineties. Now we are really starting to do it. I've heard both the mystic Andrew Harvey and the actor Terence Stamp say that same thing. It's happening and you can be part of it. Part of the solution, not the problem.

And of course, if you can't do 'It', do realise that only 5% of you is conscious. So it's hardly a surprise if you find doing 'It' is hard. What about invoking some super-force? I don't care if you believe in God, Buddha, Allah, or in nothing. For those of you who do believe in a specific religion, skip the next paragraph; for those who don't, read on.

The most ardent atheist believes in his own power for good or bad. I've treated enough of them. But what some don't realise is the power of the unconscious. I really think it is like Superman or Batman or Captain Planet. 'May the force be with you'. What's the problem with invoking that force that can accomplish things so much more easily than our blocked 5%? It's only our ego pride which says: "What a load of nonsense. I've got to do it my way, the long hard way. I don't believe in that mumbo-jumbo. I've got to suffer." That's our confused, misguided independence. But if that's the way it works for you, well and good, carry on. But if you're not fully happy, and if you do want to heal and be healed, surely invoking the power is worth a try. Einstein actually said, "I didn't achieve anything through my rational mind." I find that comment fascinating. Is it really so difficult to 'hand over'? I don't mean we should lie flat on the ground and wait for Godot. I just mean having something like the intention: "When I lay my hands on this person, may the forces of good be with me to multiply my conscious strength." UGH! Maybe not quite those words, but something that suits you. You choose. It's all within you. Start where you are.

Chapter Two
Breathing, Meditation and Calming the Mind

So, having now got used to checking your motivation and intention, it would be most helpful if you could retain your positive frame of mind and therefore help more effectively.

And how to do this? Meditation, plain and simple. Some people, very few and far between, may not need to do this. Matthew Manning considers that he 'hits the ceiling' when he meditates, and can't get on with anything. But for most of us it's a way of training ourselves to improve the quality of our own life, and therefore the lives of others.

You may not be someone who thinks about what you're thinking. Equally, you may be tremendously aware of particular thoughts: of your *belief* that you're not good enough to heal, that your mind flitters all the time and that you cannot stay centred. You may be nervous and scared, or thinking about what you're not doing and should be doing. You may wonder how on earth you decided you wanted to become a healer in the first place. You may doubt why you're reading this book, etc., etc. The real issue here is that your mind is jumping. Jumping all the time. The French have a wonderful expression which they use rather differently than we do: 'zapping'. They use it of people who keep changing channels on the television or radio. They zap the waves. And I think that's what we do with our mind. We zap into one thing, and then another, and never stay still. But if you think about it, that just may take away from the quality of the present moment. After all, what has gone, has gone. However much your head is full of past grievances, guilt and memories, they are not happening now. Equally, it does not help worrying about what has not happened yet, or what you want to make happen. Remember that song they often play on the radio? "Que sera, sera; whatever will be, will be." And yet we persist in trying to control our environment, our little world, or in trying to avoid it through escape.

Meditation is giving yourself permission to sit. And if you're one of those people who doesn't like the notion of meditation, don't meditate, just sit. I believe meditation is more than just the act of sitting. Meditation is like a revolution in this day and age when time is so very precious, when everything seems so speeded up. But if you've got as far as reading this book, you're well on the way to resolution and to turning the clock around. Time is man-made anyway. What is this thing called pressure? Why do we think that we can't forge ten minutes twice out of a day just to sit? Are we all such deep victims of the Protestant work ethic? Do we all hate ourselves so much that we don't feel we deserve to sit? Are we all such avoidance freaks that we have to keep 'doing' all the time? Are we all so guilty that we can't simply take time to have pleasure? Or are we all afraid that meditation may bring up something we don't want to know about? Or that our children will punish us because they had five minutes less of quality time? Or are we just lazy? Or even afraid of being bored?

When I give a talk to doctors or nurses, I speak knowing full well that they really are stressed and overworked. But I challenge them: I am married, have three children, work as a healer, give talks, write books, teach meditation, run a charity and study, and yet I can still find thirty minutes twice a day for sitting. I don't say this so that everyone can go, "Bully for you." I say it, because if I can, so can you. *If you choose to, you can.* About fourteen years ago, a teacher looked me straight in the eyes and said, "You should meditate." It frightened me a bit and it certainly didn't make me do so immediately. I would sit for a couple of minutes once a week or once a month and then give up. But about four years later I went to see the wonderful Mother Ama (an Indian Hindu who attained realisation at a young age). She gives her blessing with a hug. If ever there was an example of 'super-force', she has it. She hugs over a thousand people in an evening. It's quite mind-boggling! Anyway, before giving her darshan (blessing), she spoke a few precious words to the assembled crowds and I heard loudly and clearly: "You should meditate every day." I took it personally and have done so ever since. But don't despair if you don't, or if you do but not every day. It will come at the right time. Perhaps you could try a little more than is easy, and a little less than is difficult.

If you have got young children, remember the wise words: "Leave the door open." Yes, they come in and crawl all over you, interrupt, talk drivel and disturb you, but they are part of the practice . And it enhances your training.

If you are old and think you're 'past it' and can't learn anything new, that doesn't apply either. If you can breathe, you can meditate: *Breathe, you are alive* (the title of a TichNatHan book).

Breathing

I have this simple theory: if you look at new-born babies, most breathe quite happily (except in tragic circumstances). They just breathe in and out. They breathe naturally. They aren't bored. And if you look more closely you will notice that when they breathe in, their stomachs go out and when they exhale, their stomachs go in. In general they are quite happy being 'spacious' and it is only when something is genuinely wrong that they start crying. And they have no problem about doing that either. They cry because they *need* a cuddle, food, drink, or diaper changed.

And in general terms, most parents will accede to these needs. But as they get a little older, the child gets a dummy stuck in the mouth, gets scolded, goes to school, takes exams and develops hobbies, and moves further and further away from being natural. We then reach a point when we don't know how to be that child again. We've forgotten.

Have a go now and see how you breathe. Take that time. Don't rush on to the next chapter. Stop now and be in the moment: *Breathe in through the nose, throat, lungs, push your stomach out. Breathe out pulling your stomach in, up through your lungs, throat, nose and out. In brief: breathe in, stomach out, breathe out, stomach in.*

If you can't breathe through your nose, don't worry. If you can, great. If you're a singer or sports-person, you are probably already familiar with this. And some of you may find this utterly basic. For those of you who don't, mastering this simple breathing is a gateway to healing yourself and it's the start of the way to healing others. It is so simple and so important. If you can begin to incorporate this into your daily life so that you breathe three times like this every time you put on the kettle or get some coffee or get into your car or answer the phone, you will begin to breathe more life into yourself. Do breathe deeply the three times you are specifically doing this, but don't do it for too long or you might hyper-ventilate. If you wish to continue to breathe properly, just breathe at a normal pace.

A lady was once rushed to hospital with bad asthma and when I visited her, I taught her to do this. After a couple of hours she was dismissed. You might call it fluke – I would – but it just could be....'Worth a try'. And pass it on. If it's useful, use it. If not, pass on to the next thing.

Meditation

I feel very humble, giving you directions on how to meditate. There are so many forms and you can pay thousands to learn them, but these simple ones, taught me by a variety of very great masters over the years, are to me the most helpful and productive. It is with the deepest gratitude that I write these simple guidelines and hope that they may bless your healing path as they have undoubtedly blessed mine. And if you have a chance to learn meditation from a great master, go to see them, and discard the following immediately.

Instructions

1. If you are decided that this is for you and it's going to be an on-going journey, find a space in your home for *you*. Make it a sacred space, your own personal shrine. Place on it some incense or gentle aromatherapy oil, some flowers if you have time, a candle if you can be bothered, and more importantly a picture of somebody or something who/which inspires you. I don't mean some six foot hunk or topless lady, but a picture of Jesus if you're a Christian, Buddha if you're a Buddhist, or a mountain or a very old tree if you don't have a 'faith'; or choose whatever turns you on. Preferably not of Harrods as a schoolgirl once did.... You can change it if it doesn't work and go on until you find one that suits. Creating the right spot and atmosphere is a journey of discovery in itself. Equally, in this busy day and age, it is sometimes necessary to dispense with the trappings, so if you are always on the move, forget the above.

One great Tibetan master, Ato Rinpoche, spoke of his enjoyment of modern-day travel and how he had once journeyed on a long flight from Thailand to England. His neighbour on the plane persisted in giving him magazines, food, chat, etc., unable to grasp that Rinpoche was quite happy simply meditating: sitting and staring for hours on end straight ahead at the seat in front of him. How Rinpoche laughed! I am sure he was *not* bored.

2. Find a comfortable space to sit. If you can sit cross-legged on a cushion, all well and good, otherwise simply sit in a chair. What is important is that your back is straight. Not pulled up so that you are rigid, but following the natural curvature of the spine. Relax your shoulders and arms. Place your hands on your knees. Allow your mouth to be fractionally open, as if you had a grain of rice between the lips. Let the tongue rest against the palate. Fiddle about until you feel you've got it right and you're comfortable. Move again if you're not.

3. Keep your eyes open. Some people find this most peculiar, but the general idea is not that you're switching off from the world and escaping, but you're simply becoming more aware. Another reason is that there is meant to be a connection between the eyes and the soul. A third reason is to stop you going to sleep! If you truly hate keeping your eyes wide open, just allow the eyelids to drop down but don't let the eye close completely.

4. Allow yourself to feel like a mountain: a mountain is inspiring and doesn't have to exert itself to be so. Or if you prefer, think of yourself as a tiger about to pounce. It cannot pounce if it is all tense. It is elegant, alert and relaxed.

5. Let your mind settle, as mud settles at the bottom of a pond or sediment at the bottom of a bottle of wine. Notice your thoughts keep coming and going, but try not to engage in conversation with them. Watch them: 'Ah, there's a thought and oh, there's another one'. Realise that they are just thoughts and try not to follow them. Typically, if you suddenly remember you've got to go to the supermarket and buy that kilo of potatoes and that bottle of olive oil, and then you start

visualising the check-out register and remember you've run out of cash and begin to worry whether you have got your credit card on you, then at the point when you remember you're meant to be meditating, you should come back and 'be here now'. Don't get angry because you've drifted off. That serves no useful purpose. Just notice that you're breathing out. Not even that *you* are breathing out. Just breathe out.

6. And keep on coming back to the outbreath. Try and allow a sense of spaciousness so that your thoughts are like waves but you are part of the ocean, or your thoughts are like clouds and you are part of the sky. The clouds come and go but the sky is always there, even if you don't always see it!

And that is it.

To me meditation is the most powerful healing tool of all. It beats anything anyone can give you and it builds up the more you do it. If you do it when you're well, it will build up a database for when you're not. If you're not well now, start building the database straightaway. It is about getting used to being, the most precious gift of all. If you're in America and you go on a course with Jon Kabat-Zinn, a famous doctor who teaches all his patients to meditate, you have to agree to do so for forty-five minutes twice a day for six weeks. He finds that at the end, people don't want to stop. I'm much more genteel, back in England, and recommend you try and start with between ten and twenty minutes twice a day. Have a go. 'Worth a try'.

Chapter Three
Visualisation

Some people can't sit still for more than a few seconds. This really interferes with meditation! Once again I would urge you to develop the ability, even if you have to try and try again. But if you can't, don't despair! There are other methods.

Visualisations, or whatever trendy 'name of the day' is being used for the same thing, abound in their variety and effectiveness. They are another form of meditation and, once again, another form of mind training. If by now you're wondering why we're concentrating on all this mumbo-jumbo when you want to get on with healing, it's because it's part and parcel of developing your innate ability to heal. The purer your mind, the purer the healing. I don't wish to become heavy or too deeply philosophical but one line has stuck with me since I heard it. It was this: "Doesn't a nightmare or good dream feel as real when you wake up as your day-to-day reality?"

Perhaps what we perceive as real isn't quite so. Perhaps we are attached too much to what *we* perceive, the way *we* see things. If we're stuck in a bad frame of mind, we tend to stay stuck unless we dull it with avoidance or escapism. If we could become aware of where our mind is stuck and use tricks to 'shake off the negativity', wouldn't that be most helpful? Our moods seem to be so thick and gluey. What if we trained ourselves to lighten up? I can't talk about the qualities of light in terms of physics but it makes sense that darkness is heavier and lightness is lighter.

When I was quite young, I heard the joke about a huge football match held after dark with floodlights on. The crowds were roaring and the teams were playing when suddenly the lights went off. No engineer could make them work, nothing could be done. Finally the organisers called out to the crowds and asked: "Is there anyone in the audience who can help us?" A Chinese gentleman stepped forward. "I can," he replied. The organisers were doubtful but with no other suggestions, they thought they should let him have a go. So he walked to the centre of the playing field, stood there with a microphone, and called out: "Does everyone here want the match to go on?" The audience roared approvingly. "Then please put your hands up in the air." So the audience put their hands up in the air, and the lights went on. When asked to explain this, the Chinese gentleman replied, "It is an old Chinese proverb: *'Many hands make light work'*."

I have no idea why such a banal joke stays with me but think it might be the attraction of magic. There is so much day-to-day-ness in our lives, and yet so much magic too if we allow it or perceive it. I also like the idea of community spirit. I keep on trying to persuade the doctors to do group workshops on a weekly basis. Why? Because so many people today are lonely and cut off. All the healing in the world isn't going to stop their sense of isolation, but if they were to realise that they're not alone, then they would feel a lot better. I know so many people who could be so useful to the community, but whose talents are wasted.

I would like to encourage you to do this visualisation. Many people have remarked to me on its effectiveness, and two people in particular have reported great results after doing it once a day for several weeks. Curiously, both had suffered from ME (Chronic Fatigue Syndrome) for a number of years. When I last spoke to them, the first had recovered to such a degree that she had become a postman (or rather, postwoman) whilst the other, after ten years of being stuck at home, had embarked on a course in reflexology. I only mention these examples to encourage you, realising two people's experience is only anecdotal evidence.

However, I can promise you that I have used this visualisation at numerous workshops and it has helped many people to release pent-up emotion.

THE VISUALISATION

Before you start, please consider whether you might find it easier to record this, reading it aloud while running a tape and then playing it back when you have twenty minutes' free time (or when you carve out the time!). If you do tape it, make sure to speak slowly.

- Don't worry if you don't 'see' what you visualise. Thinking it is just as effective.

- If, during the course of the visualisation, you are asked to think about something and have a problem with it, don't panic, just notice that you have a block and think about it later.

- If, for a particular section, two suggestions come to mind, use one now and the other later when you do the visualisation again.

Lie down comfortably with your eyes closed and let your body relax.

Imagine a ball of brilliant white light above your head; it is made of rainbow light, not solid at all but of a beautiful translucent rainbow quality. See it shining brightly.

In fact, it shines so brightly, it makes you want to climb into it and sit down. You're entering it alone but you can take a comfortable chair with you, or if you prefer, mould the earth within it to fit you perfectly. Just ensure that you are sitting in the most comfortable position possible in the ball of brilliant white light. When you're settled, I would like you to breathe in as deeply as possible and release with a noisy sigh.

Now, I would like you to think of the perfect view for you: a view of nature; of the sun and sea or mountains or meadows or forests; whatever you prefer. Really see the view, examining it from the top of the sky to the ground. Spend some time doing so. And then let it expand to the left and to the right, and finally, imagining you have eyes in the back of your head, to the back of you. Imagine you have a 360-degree view and are completely surrounded by this perfect vista. And then I would like you to breathe in as deeply as you can and release with a noisy sigh.

Next, I would like you to imagine your favourite smell: Chanel number five or lily of the valley, whatever is your perfect smell, and place it in the ball of light.

And then I would like you to imagine your perfect taste: mango sorbet or chocolate or vintage Champagne, whatever is your perfect taste, and place that in the ball of light.

And then I would like you to imagine your perfect sound: Beethoven's Number Nine, trickling water or whatever it is, and place that in the ball of light.

And then I would like you to imagine what feels perfect to your touch: a baby's bottom, a piece of moss, whatever it is, and place that in the ball of light.

And so I would like you to place all these perfect senses in your ball of light, which becomes your sacred space.

So your sacred space contains all the senses which are perfect for you: your perfect view, smell, taste, sound and touch. Breathe them all in as deeply as you can and release with a noisy sigh.

All that is missing now is the perfect feeling. So if you can, I would like you to go back to a moment in childhood when you went swimming in the sea for the first time or won a three-legged race at school or found a four leaf clover. Whatever it was, it made you feel so happy, your cheeks were red, you were bursting with joy and felt completely carefree. Place that feeling in the ball of light.

Then I would like you to go to a moment such as when you first fell in love: that special time when you could have danced all night; when all the lyrics in all the songs related directly to you; when you had boundless energy; when you smiled constantly and thought that only you knew what it was like to be so much in love. In fact, you felt like a Mills and Boon or Harlequin novel and thought it would last forever. Place that feeling in the ball of light as well.

This is your sacred space, your healing space, full of the perfect things for you. It is true that the feeling does not necessarily last forever, neither does that boundless energy. BUT the ball of light **does** *last forever and it is constantly replenishing itself, full of never-ending love and healing.*

And so I would like you to imagine an opening in the crown of your head, the width of the stem of a flower and leading to the ball of light. From that ball flows a drop of light: your healing light.

So imagine a drop of this light flowing into your head, and then another drop of light, until a steady trickle of this perfect healing light flows from the ball into the inside of your head, healing you as it pours in. Imagine it pouring down through your throat, through your chest and lungs, down through your stomach, through the reproductive organs and down through your legs to your feet.

Imagine the earth cracking open beneath you, and then out from the soles of your feet pours your pain (physical, mental, emotional or spiritual), in the form of black oil or manure.

And again, above your head, see the light pouring into your head, down your neck, shoulders, arms and fingers and down your spine and spinal cord, spreading across your vertebrae. Down through the coccyx and down the back of your legs to your toes, pushing down and out all your pain, in the form of black oil or manure.

And again, see the light cascading through you. If you like cleaning, you could imagine a scrubbing brush of gentle healing light, cleaning out the most resistant blocks, reaching the parts that no-one has reached before. Let go of the resistance. Let the light liquefy you. Let it reach the parts that no-one else can. Let it flow down through the front of you and the back of you and through the middle, inside and out, really pushing your resistance out through the soles of your feet as you watch the manure or black oil pour out.

And one last time, really see the light flowing through you like a waterfall of healing light until the last residue of pain is pushed down and out. The earth closes up and you thank the earth for taking your pain. You are left in the light, feeling perhaps a little like the astronauts when they were bouncing on the moon...

How are you feeling now? Calmer? I hope so, and I hope you use it again and again, adapting it to your situation. You certainly don't need to keep it the same every time you do it. You can also simplify it as much as you want and use a brief version in the middle of your day.

For those of you who want to heal others, start using the light on them. You can't always help people in the way you may want. For example if you pass by an accident and see someone who is injured, you may not have the expertise to bind their wounds but you can easily send them the light and bathe them in it. Better than nothing and *worth a try*. When I was in India, somebody suggested I bathe the beggars there in light. I couldn't always give money, so it was something I *could* do. At least it made me feel better.

This reminds me of a day when I was practising sending the light to people on a busy commuter train in Bombay. I was sitting innocently doing my little bit when I noticed a saddhu (someone who has given up the worldly life to devote themselves to spiritual attainment) at the other end of the carriage staring at me. He nodded, winked and started laughing and laughing. He might have been off his rocker, but I like to believe that he was feeling the light and pointing that out to me. Delete this last paragraph if you think that notion is too wacky for you...Who knows? It's certainly more useful than sending out negative thoughts.

So, meditation *and* visualisation? You may find that you prefer practising one mode and not the other, or might want a variation on a theme, and that's absolutely fine. And if you find that you have enough on your plate just practising the meditation and/or visualisation, stop here. But if you would like to develop further, I would encourage you to read on.

Chapter Four
Exchanging Yourself
for Another

If you really want to magnify the effectiveness of your healing, you will want to develop the practice of exchange. One master used just this one practice for forty years, but if you get bored, remember what we said about 'zapping the channels'.

It is incredibly easy to describe the practice of exchange but very hard to *really* do it and keep on doing it, so if you don't succeed at first, try and try again. First, some background on why it is so important.

It does seem to me that most of the problems in the world come from our being stuck in our own spot, believing we are all-important and that our viewpoint is the be-all and end-all. When somebody hurts us, our usual reaction (inward or outward) is: 'That person. How *dare* they behave that way? How *dare* they be so horrible? I'm right, and I just know that they're wrong'. Or we might feel so superior (or inferior) that we refuse to engage in the issue at all, and instead bury it in our subconscious. Or we might take out our anger on someone else, usually someone smaller than ourselves and perfectly innocent. Whatever the comment levelled at us, the pain comes from our attachment to the way we interpret it; the way we care for ourselves first of all, rather than allowing in the other's view point. And we stay stuck in our own view; often retaining the imprint of hurt long after the issue is resolved. We love a little less and withdraw a little more. We don't let go. We hang on to something that is long gone. We forget that, in spite of ourselves, everything changes.

Suppose you turn to your friend and ask, "Do you think this shirt looks right on me for tomorrow?" And the friend says, "No, I think you'd look better in that blue one." You might immediately think that she doesn't want you to look good, doesn't have good clothes sense, regret having asked her in the first place, and know anyway that she is wrong and you are right. You're locked into your own way of seeing things. If you could allow time for a little pause, you might notice that your friend is actually going to carry on and explain: "Andrew is going to wear that same outfit tomorrow and I don't think you would be happy if he stole the show, since you're the main speaker." I know this example is trivial and you probably wouldn't react in this way at all, but is it really very different from politicians on the television or radio? Certainly British ones. One day it's all about sleaze and MPs lambasting the party in office for their bad behaviour, priding themselves on how squeaky clean they are; and then the next day, that party is out of office and is busy lambasting the newly elected party on the same issues. I always used to listen to the radio, thinking it was important to 'keep up' with the news. I was once almost enticed into it when a politician I knew was accused of wild philandering. He was news and I could have sold my story, for I had been witness to him being thrown into a bathful of gelatine on his twenty-first birthday. Wouldn't the tabloids have loved that? I understood how easy it was to fall into the trap of trivia, the trap of joining the wagon train. I realised then that I was one of thousands who were actually encouraging journalists and politicians to continue their games and that I was wanting to join them, to be important, to validate myself. So I switched off, and am now short of witty repartee at the dinner table.

Of course, my single response is not going to change the world, and it is certain that the world does not change easily. A friend who had spent seven years on retreat told me she had gone into the retreat with politicians arguing, and come out of it to find different politicians, but still arguing about the same issues. There was no change. What's more, she'd missed a war! They say too that in caves in China there are meditators who have been meditating since the turn of the century. When some of them came out of their cave and were approached by – you guessed it – journalists, they turned round and enquired 'Mao? Mao who?'. From that perspective, maybe our problems are not so vast. And because many hands do make light work, perhaps we can start with our internal cleansing. Maybe we can begin to loosen up; do that old thing of going up in a helicopter and looking down at ourselves. Don't we look small?

Yet we still remain attached to our pain, to our way of seeing things. So therefore I for one can see the logic in trying to train my mind to go beyond its blocked horizons. Boy, does it need training!

So, what to do, what to do? Start now and have a go.

EXCHANGING YOURSELF FOR ANOTHER

Imagine someone you know well standing in front of you. Someone you want to help. Someone in pain. Whatever kind of pain, it doesn't matter. Sit for a few minutes and just look at them. See what they look like, what they're wearing, their complexion, the spot on their nose, their unpolished shoes. Don't do anything; just get in touch with their appearance.

After a few minutes, begin to feel what it might be like to be them. Imagine what it is like to be in their body, to have their life, their feelings. Try and begin to see it from their perspective rather than yours. Imagine having their problem.

As the wall begins to break down between you and the other person, you might find yourself understanding them a little more and focusing more on them rather than yourself. As this happens, allow yourself to breathe in their pain as black smoke and breathe out light onto them. Don't worry if you can't see the smoke, it's the idea behind it that counts, the act of breathing in their pain. So breathe in their pain and breathe out the light. Keep on doing it.

If your mind wanders, don't worry, but return to the focus point when you can. And if you feel you have done enough, move on to anyone else you would like to help. A tramp in your backyard, a refugee in Kosovo, Clinton, the Monicas (did you know that people named Monica have set up a self-help group?), the divorced couple up the road, the man in Africa who gets up in the morning and goes out with a bucket looking for rainclouds.... And then, if you can, extend that view to all those in the world with that sort of pain, all the people in the world who are bereaved, all the people in the world who've suffered, all the people who are angry; breathe in all their pain and breathe out white light into all the world.

Finally, let your mind settle, using the simple meditation practice in chapter two, and just let go.

That's it. The formal way. But of course, I'm sure you realise you can use this whenever you want. If you find yourself arguing with your partner, breathe in their pain, their 'separateness' and breathe out light. If you find you've got a major block such as anger or jealousy or hatred, place that in front of you, visualising it as you wish: a block of coal, an ice-cube, a burning red ball, whatever you prefer, and breathe that in as black smoke and breathe out light onto it. If someone rings you about their sick mother, breathe in their mother's pain as black smoke and breathe out light onto them, and do it for the caller as well. If you're in the supermarket and a baby is bawling and the mother is waiting desperately in the checkout queue, breathe in their discomfort and breathe out light onto them. It works. And you won't catch it, though that is a common fear. I still find that I resist breathing in the distress of someone's cold. Something to do with that old habit of turning away when a person sneezes.

Funniest of all is that if you're feeling lousy but manage to rouse yourself out of your apathy for long enough to concentrate on someone else's problem, you begin to feel better, and even energised. It stops you falling into the trap of your ego, which is your focus on yourself. What is that ego anyway? Where is it? If you chop up your body bit by bit, where will you find that bit of you that is you? Is it in your leg, your arm, your cerebellum? Go on, I challenge you. Doctors too have shown in the latest round of research that they cannot find that thing in your body which makes you lift up your arm. That 'thing' is definitely not there. Very interesting....

So, even if you haven't had the experience which leads you to believe there is more to you than the eye can see, perhaps you can allow for the common sense value of these last few chapters. They are all for you, for anybody, and you do not need to be a superman to start. You are one, anyway. Just keep training. A la Diana Ross, "What the world needs now, is love, sweet love."

Anything external is a reflection of something going on within us. We cannot cut ourselves off from others, though my ego would truly love to! So it follows that what we change for good in ourselves has an external effect as well. The mystic Andrew Harvey used to say, "A butterfly in Yucatan affects the way we breathe here." I'm sure you all know that, but if you're not the type to join Friends of the Earth and go on marches or reach into your pockets for Live Aid, perhaps you might like to start with yourself. *Worth a try.* Forget about this compassion thing if you find it difficult. If you prefer, start because *you* want to feel better. The rest will follow. We are all interconnected.

Chapter Five
The Ideal Situation

So finally we reach the point where we talk about conventional hands-on healing. I do hope you understand why I have gone on so much about other forms of healing. It's because if you master them, I doubt very much you will need to use your hands. Jesus didn't automatically lay his hands on people. And when he did heal physical ailments, it wasn't necessarily by pointing to the physical cause: "Get up, thy sins are forgiven" is a very interesting example. Note the connection between mind and body. Could it be true that 'It' is all in the mind'? People at Lourdes are not healed through hands-on healing. Nor do great Tibetan or Indian masters lay their hands on people. Yet many of them heal.

In my practice, I often use the trick of pretending to be someone's dark side, the bit they don't want to be. You know, the bit that wants everything now, that hates themselves for not being kind, successful, loving, wealthy, or unable to give up the addiction or whatever it is. So I stand in front of them and ask them to whitewash me. To paint me white. A light sort of white, nothing heavy. And they feel it. They can really feel themselves doing it. They can really feel the power. These aren't trained healers or psychic surgeons; they are just so-called ordinary people. It gives me such pleasure to let them feel the power of their mind. Yet it's no different from the times you walk into a room and feel the tension because somebody there has had an argument. How many people do you know who say they bought a house because it 'had a good feeling'? And how many others do you know who didn't buy a house for the opposite reason? Loads of people. It is not unusual at all.

THE SPACE

Of course, it follows that for us less consciously enlightened beings, it would increase the effectiveness if we had the right space and time to concentrate our mind and heal. If, however, you are literally faced with someone who's sprained an ankle and you can offer healing, it is more important to simply hold his or her hands rather than have that ideal space. Equally, if you are giving a talk, it is rare for a couch to be provided for your demonstration 'client'.

Nevertheless, if you can, try to set up your ideal situation. I love working in my room and although I have hired practice rooms in clinics from time to time, I have always come back to the room in my home. Why? Because I practice meditation in it and because it has been blessed by great masters. I regularly space clear it (another topic) and I also burn incense before patients come in. I find this most inspiring, and so do most people. Even my accountant commented that my account books "smelled sweeter than those of any other of her clients!" So, if you do have a room you can keep for healing purposes, all to the good.

THE TOOLS

If you don't have a room, it is a good idea to have a portable couch. Make sure that it suits your height so that you're not bending down all the time. If you're not comfortable, you won't be sufficiently relaxed for effective healing. When I first started, I used to end up in the most awkward situations: cramps in my legs; trying to stretch across beds at all sorts of obtuse angles; it doesn't work. I suppose it did make me aware of pain, but I think more of mine than theirs! Not such a hot idea.

Make sure the couch is wide enough to support the arms flat by the side of the body. Many osteopaths' couches are narrower than that and, although it is a matter of personal choice, I recommend the wider type for your patient's comfort.

If you can't afford a couch, don't despair; you can use a chair, but try to get one with a canvas back so you can heal through the cotton. I never find this situation ideal, but there are some patients who are too sick to get onto a couch. And some find it too uncomfortable to lean forward so you can reach their backs easily. Another possible position is to ask the patient to sit back-to-front on a straight-backed chair. That can work if you're healing casually and they aren't too uncomfortable. Remember, therefore, it's all in the mind, and you need to find the most practical option that works best for the two of you.

THE PREPARATION

I always meditate before I treat anyone in a formal situation. It really matters to me because I just don't like laying hands on anyone before I've cleared up a bit of my inner junk. Naturally that wouldn't stop me in an emergency: on those occasions, invoking 'the force' suffices. I leave this for you to mull upon. It's my view point, yours may be different.

People need only to take off their shoes, and if they're sitting down, I don't even expect that. Nor do I ask them to remove their watches and jewellery unless it's heavy and clunky. The simpler the better.

I'm not going into the legalities of treating people. I will leave that to the numerous organisations which will help you out. What I will do is to concentrate on the healing act and describe my own experience.

BREATHING, INTENTION AND INVOCATION

The patient is now lying on the couch, on their back, knees bent if they prefer. Make sure they are warm enough, and comfortable. Their eyes are closed, and I ask them to take three deep breaths as in Chapter Two. I take the same breath as they do, so our breathing is synchronised for those few moments. I then voice the intention for the healing: "May this healing be as powerful as possible and last for as long as possible." Since some counselling or listening has gone on before the patient reaches the couch, I voice further intentions according to circumstances. For example: "May you intend that the blocks to your healing be removed. May you really stop feeling guilty about the bullying you did as a child/feeling vindictive because of the bullying you received as a child/feeling angry because your husband ran off with your best friend/etc, etc." The list is sadly infinite. I also ask the patient to silently add to themselves any other intentions they have.

Then I play some gentle music and stand at the head of the couch. I invoke that the highest power of love be within me, that that unconscious force for good take over and do the healing for me, that my ego let go. When you practise this, please do go to the highest source of love.

I know that many of you may have guides or feel your angels. Invoke them too if that is your path, but please be careful. It isn't that they aren't necessarily working for the highest good, it is just that you don't know for sure. They might not even know for sure. I think most of us would admit to being quite frequently deluded, so who's to say that when you die and end up as a guide, spirit or angel that you aren't at some level still deluded. The healer Betty Shine always makes me laugh about her 'mischievous' friends who appear out of nowhere and unpack her cases whilst she's out of the hotel room so when she returns there's chaos.

Betty Shine is a healer whom I greatly respect and her way is her way, and very successful, but to most of us aspiring healers, it might be better perhaps to play safe. Why not go to the top, when for once it's just as easy to do so? A lot easier than talking to the chairman of Monsanto or BT, I bet. Please simply be cautious. There are many false gurus and gods around. I hear of new sects all the time. For those who have an authentic teacher, that is great too.

TIMING

It is imperative that you work out how to use the time allotted. Many new healers spend twenty minutes on one hand position, and then there is no time left. That doesn't work. Nor does stopping half-way through. You need to complete the treatment, and you need to know that you can do so. Check that the patient has got twenty minutes or an hour, whatever it is you want to offer, and make sure they won't get a parking ticket or the sack if you over-run. If you must over-run, do so by five minutes maximum. That's the one and only order I'll give you! If you can't work out the time schedule for your sessions, get somebody to do the maths for you. If you use x number of positions, you have x minutes per position, and make sure the clock is around. Not for you to observe obsessively of course, but just make sure it's there. As you gain confidence, you'll know where to place your hands for longer periods, and it will come naturally. You can move out of time to the point where you feel as if you've spent a second on healing, and the recipient feels like you've spent an eternity.

ACTION (AT LAST!)

And then move into action. You'll see below the list of body positions I recommend. I do not stick to them but this is the general format. I use it because it's simple and effective. If you're concerned and worried about whether you've put your hand positions in the right place, it will detract from the healing. Just keep the touch very gentle. Simplicity is all, both for you and the patient.

Caution: the diagrams show the hand positions as clearly as possible, but I always treat people fully clothed and with a cotton blanket to cover them. This is less inhibiting for them.

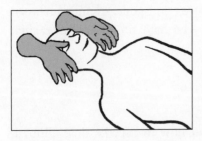 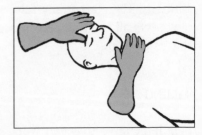

1&2. Ask the patient to lie on their back (supine). Stand at their head with hands out in the air over the side of the patient's head to make a very gentle contact, then move to their right and place your left hand over the crown of the head and the right hand above the throat (not touching in either case).

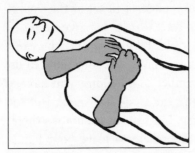 

3. With both hands, gently touch over the heart centre.

4. With both hands, gently touch over the stomach and spleen.

5. With your left hand, gently touch the right shoulder while you touch the right wrist with your right hand.

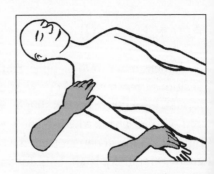

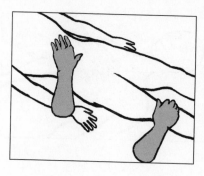

6. Gently touch the stomach with your left hand and the right knee with your right.

7. Carefully move around to the other side of the couch, keeping hand contact on the right knee, then place both hands gently on left knee.

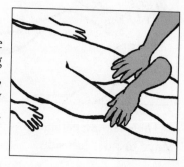

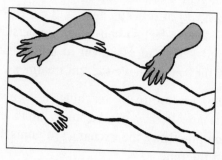

8. Gently place left hand on knee, right hand on stomach.

9. Gently place both hands on stomach.

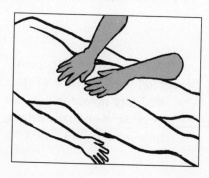

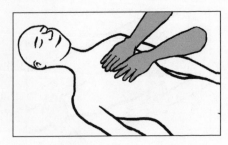

10. Gently place both hands over and on the heart.

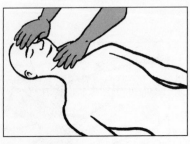

11. Place left hand over throat, right hand over third eye, not touching in either case.

Then ask the patient to turn over and lie on their front (prone). Move to their left side.

I have a friend who's an inventor in Austria and I keep asking him to make a machine which will turn people over without their having to make the effort. I always feel so bad when the person is relaxed or even asleep and I have to ask them to move, but there is no way around it if they are to have the full treatment.

Once they are lying prone, you are really reaching in deeply. Notice where your thoughts are. If they are negative, think of something inspiring. Keep on practising the exchange of yourself for another. Keep on raising the tone.

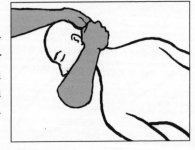

12. Place your hands gently touching over the back of their head (my favourite position because everyone carries a whole load of junk in there).

13. Moving carefully round to the patient's left side, place your left hand gently touching over the top of their head, with your right hand on the back of their neck, opposite the throat.

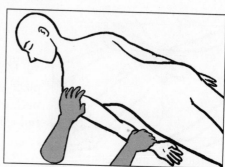

14. Left hand on left shoulder, right hand on left wrist.

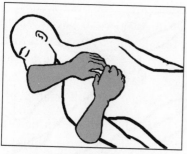

15. Both hands cupped over heart, gently touching.

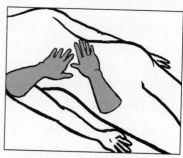

16. Both hands gently touching over the stomach and spleen.

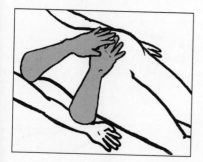

17. Both hands gently touching over the coccyx.

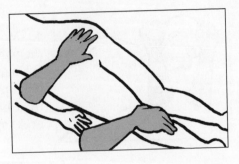

18. Left hand on the coccyx, right hand on the back of the left knee.

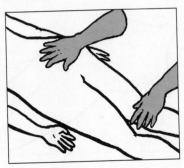

19. Move round the couch and place your left hand on the back of the right knee and your right hand on the coccyx.

20. Place both hands gently on the coccyx.

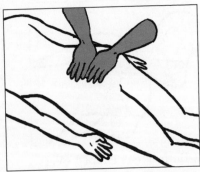

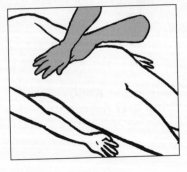

21. Place both hands gently on the stomach and spleen.

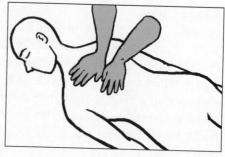

22. Place both hands over the heart, gently touching.

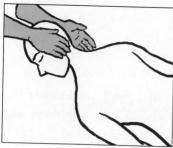

23. Place left hand over back of neck, right hand over top of head, not touching.

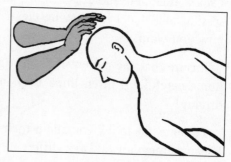

24. Moving round to the patient's head, place both hands over the top of the head, not touching.

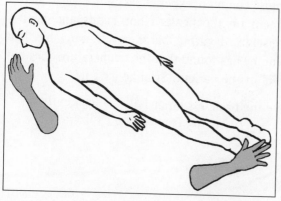

25. It is now time to complete the healing, yours and the patient's. When you finish at the head you will probably be wondering if you have done

25 continued

enough. You may even be feeling guilty that your thoughts were so mundane or unhelpful. To counteract that feeling, you can stand at the side of the couch and place both your hands outstretched a good 7.5 cms (3 inches) from the patient's head and toes, and radiate light into them through your hands. Wash them in the light. You can also breathe deeply three times and really be as conscious as possible of the practice of exchange. I recommend using symbols at this point if you so choose. More on that in the next chapter.

The aftermath

I always allow the patient to come round gently and urge them to sit up slowly and take their time while I leave the room and wash my hands. I always wash my hands if I can, and if I can't, I shake them. For me, it is a sign that I have finished the healing session and that I like having clean hands. You can interpret it how you want.

Ensure that the patient feels all right and that they will drive home carefully. I often think they might get arrested for drunk driving!

Patients like to tell you about their experiences. I love listening because they are always different and always different from mine. One of the most common experiences is the 'heat factor'. Many people comment on the healer's hot hands and healers often notice it themselves. I gather Matthew Manning has had tests done on him and he has found that the temperature does not change either for him or the patient. Strange isn't it?

So there you have the basic essentials.

Chapter Six
Symbols and Faith

The New Age is most certainly serving its purpose. It's set so many people on a search. It's got so many doing therapy this and therapy that, and don't forget the new brand-x therapy, and I am not knocking it. But what I think happens is that once you start treating people, *if you are genuine,* you want to heal more effectively. So you study and study and study, and spend any money you have earned on more courses! And still there is the need to develop further. You still cannot heal all the people who come and see you...

There is so much jargon in the world, apart from the New Age variety, and it seems mostly used to patent some proprietary item. You only have to switch on a computer and access clip art to be deluged with different images, all of them someone's property, even if the owner lets you use them. Healing is no different. Everyone seems to want to appropriate it and say, "Do it this way" or "You must do that or it won't work." People even put copyrights on their particular variety. They promote their jargon and often suggest you use their symbols to make the healing work.

But why use a symbol if it is meaningless to you? It is the meaning which makes it work. And what does a symbol mean? Different things to different people. People advertise week-ends 'unveiling the secret path to inner healing' or 'how to achieve tantra in 24 hours' or 'the symbol to heal the corn on your big toe for only $1000'. And there is all this hoo-ha about Reiki masters. Properly trained masters paid at least £5000 to graduate and completed their training over a number of years. Now you can 'become a Reiki master in two days for only £50'. You'll learn your symbols and may start teaching them to someone else straightaway, but what is it that lies behind the action? What was your motivation – or your teacher's? How much of it was money, and was impatience a part of it?

So really, could not all these copyrights be born out of fear and greed? What has ownership got to do with healing? Who owns love? Who can sell love? This is where the zealots and I part company, and I am sorry if I cause offence. I cannot find it within me to believe that if you have lived in Timbuktu and not heard the word 'Reiki' or 'Jesus' or 'Allah', that you are not going to be able to *love or heal*. That cannot be so. This love is always within us waiting to be uncovered. I do not say that you are not fortunate to have your particular background and experience, nor that one way will not suit you better than another (as discussed in Chapter Seven), just that to impose your views as being the only valid ones is more than a little dubious.

For a number of years I have felt that the New Age was the precursor to a return to religion and was so pompously pleased when the (London) Daily Telegraph's headline read in May 1999: '*Watch Out for the Latest Trend: Religion*'. It continued: '*Marketers scanning the horizon of the 21st century would be well advised to tune their radar to religion*'....'*Mr. Hall attributed the change partly to the fact that science and religion were no longer seen as incompatible*'.

In his book *The Rebirth of Nature* Rupert Sheldrake discusses how people's ideas about their connection with the natural world have changed: the Protestant Reformation removed some of the survivals of the pagan sense of connectedness, and the scientific revolution in the 17th Century advanced the idea of a mechanical universe. The Industrial Revolution in the West crystallised the feeling of separation. Before, people thought they were part of God/the universe, and since then they have felt they have ruled the universe.

But for those of you who find religion problematic, I am not talking about dogma or blind faith. Towards the end of his career, Carl Jung was asked if he believed in God. He replied that he did not believe, he knew. What I am advocating is a return to 'knowing'. Knowing that there is more than meets the eye, whether you use your intuition, psychology, philosophy or religion to develop it. As faith or 'knowing' becomes understanding, one needs less faith anyway.

I remember hearing that a gentleman in Scotland quite regularly experienced the stigmata (when you bleed from the wounds of Christ), and was extremely frustrated because he had no faith whatsoever and just wanted to get on with his life. Poor man! There was also the case of a farmer in Devon who was renowned as a healer. People would come from miles to see him. He would be milking the cows and tell the visitor to 'hang on a minute' whilst he finished his work. He would then wipe his hands on an old cloth and sit the visitor on the same stool to give the healing. It worked and his fame grew! He had no 'training' whatsoever and he used no symbols. This is just another instance showing that it is wrong to think that because you have no faith you cannot heal.

You can understand this if you simply accept the law of cause and effect: what you sow is what you reap. To put it another way, what you did before has led you to where you are now, and what you do now will lead you to where you are going. I won't embroider on that: it's too broad a subject.

Religion cannot therefore always be a prerequisite to healing. The reason I mention 'that word' is because it could give you a *training* in the development of love. Most religions have been around a long time and should be able to offer the guidelines of experience (though sadly, nowadays even that needs checking for motivation and to avoid sects). So how better to improve ourselves than to turn inwards and develop the study of compassion? The thing about compassion is that, at its most developed, it obviates the need for any other external symbol or tool. It also leads you out of suffering because it concentrates your attention on others. It surprises me how people will always agree that it is more pleasurable to give a present to someone than to receive one. Isn't that odd? Do you not agree that real happiness can only come from making others happy? Do you not find that, if you had all those things you wanted in life, you would still want more? Doesn't love fill that bottomless gap? Although you might find temporary respite in other methods of therapy, the real healing will come from within. The more compassion you feel, the more you exude it to others and the more benefit they feel.

If you have mastered the contents of the previous chapters and put them into practice, I don't think there is a need for symbols: you are training in compassion. If you have *truly* mastered the contents of those chapters, let me know and I'm on my way to you for a treatment right now!

However if you do want to use symbols, here are a few pointers.

Those who have studied Reiki will have learnt to use particular symbols. Use them as you have been taught and see if they work. It won't happen overnight, but Reiki is a powerful healing force and I am sure some of you have felt results.

If you're a Christian, making the sign of the cross is extremely powerful. During World War II, my mother was evacuated to a convent in Staffordshire. She was only eight. One night she woke up having seen a ghost. The nuns came running to check on her and they didn't deny her sighting. They made this point: "Make the sign of the cross. If it's a bad ghost it will run away. If it's a good ghost, you've got nothing to fear." That story has always stayed with me. I often notice that I cross myself, almost unconsciously, if I am treating a Christian patient.

If you're a Buddhist or a Moslem or a Hindu, you might use a mantra to 'protect your mind' from negativity; and very useful they are too.

If you have no faith, it's a different matter. You simply won't believe that the above are able to help you. Yet the fact that you have picked up this book suggests there is something in it for you, and the fact you have got this far suggests that it is touching some chord. Could it be that you have some kind of hope? As my teacher says: "Is it like when you go to hospital? You go to hospital because you have the hope that you will get better." In the same way, you are reading about healing because you have the hope that you can develop that 'It'. Developing the 'It' is none other than developing that compassion within you.

If you *can't* feel it, and if you *can't* believe that such a thing exists, then try 'doing' all the past chapters and even try using a symbol if there is one which appeals to you. If all else fails, try doing affirmations. For that, read Louise Hay's book. Many, many people have found that very helpful. And if at first the affirmations don't work, keep on trying. I recommend that people persist. *Avec de la patience, tout arrive* (everything comes with patience). Those who do persist invariably feel better. First have hope, then use intention, and carry on with the practice of meditation and visualisation. This will get you out of the void; it can but lead to success. *Worth a try*. And if at first you don't succeed, try and try again. You don't want to stay stuck where you are. (Or do you?).

I bet that after six months of doing all the things we've talked about, you will begin to develop faith. Not in a symbol, and not necessarily in a religion, but you will start to develop faith in yourself – confidence. This isn't the confidence that cracks under duress, but the confidence that comes from being indestructible.

It reminds me of one of Jean de La Fontaine's fables (le chene et le roseau). The gist of the fable is that once upon a time there was a big oak tree which loomed over a little reed. He used to tell the reed how to behave and rejoiced in showing off his size and strength. "I'm so big and strong and you're such a little weed." One day a storm blew and the oak tree was felled to the ground. Dead. The reed was bent by the wind, shrinking to the earth, but when the sun came out, the reed arose too.

I love that story.

What you're trying to touch into is the indestructible self-confidence of compassion. That is the one thing that can never go wrong.

If you keep on practising and keep on developing that confidence, you will come to a point where you feel the love. You will start to develop your inner voice. You will start to know what is true and what isn't. You will be able to follow your heart. I am not denying that you might make mistakes and think that your head is your heart, but even those errors are par for the course. If things always go right, you learn nothing. We learn from our pain and mistakes. So...

Follow your heart! *Yabadabadoo*!

Chapter Seven
Others' Styles,
or Choose Your Own New One

When people start healing, they most often do so because it is the start of a journey into self-discovery and the power within. This often comes about as the result of a lack of confidence, or the desire to search for something beyond the ordinary drudge of daily life, something with true meaning. A way of being helpful. Forgive me, please, those who don't fall into this category (and those who do!). Anyway, as I've already mentioned, nothing happens by chance, and if you have started healing or are about to do so, I am sure it is because you have already found the 'right connection' for you at this moment. Yes, all roads lead to Rome (i.e., the heart), but there are so many different ways to get there. To put it another way, we may all go to the supermarket to buy cheese but some of us will buy Brie, others Cheddar, others Gouda and yet others will choose among umpteen more varieties. So people really need to trust that if they are happy with one form of healing and it works for them, all is well and good. If it doesn't taste good, they may want to try a different kind. Equally, they might want to dabble with a bit of this before going on to a bit of that, until they decide that they really do want to stick with a particular variety because it seems to go down best and easiest. There is no 'right' way. There is no 'one' way. There is only the way. Back to remembering your motivation before you start.

Many people have been led to Matthew Manning, perhaps one of the most famous hands-on healers in the world. To me he will always be immortalised by the phrase: "I wouldn't know a chakra if it hit me walking down the street" (do you still say that Matthew?). He teaches basic, down-to-earth, completely honest, no frills stuff: 'love and go out and do it'. His no-nonsense approach is based on the fact that everyone is ordinary and yet everyone can heal, so you shouldn't have to pay a fortune to learn one of your own naturally innate skills. He's been barking out the same message for years and years. He suggests, 'do it with your hands', because that's the way he has found it works for him, but, as we've seen already, that isn't the only way. I remember going to one of the London 'Mind, Body & Spirit' festivals where he performed hands-on healing on two hundred participants whilst Denise Linn did a visualisation and Tim Wheater played his marvellous flute. It was clear they could see things the general audience couldn't, but the gist of it was that all three forms of healing had the same effect. So good was it that I forgot where I had parked my car.

If you were to go to Lency Spezzano's healing workshops, it would be an altogether different experience. She has developed a form of healing through the right eye. Perhaps it sounds wacky to some, but it is very powerful. By simply looking at someone's right eye she manages to reach into those parts of you that you may not consciously want to be reached, and this allows healing to happen. She works with groups of two hundred, but is equally at home on a one-to-one basis with multiply disabled persons and critically ill children. The eye is often said to have a direct connection with the heart. Once again, she doesn't keep this method to herself or sell it to the highest bidder. If you feel like it, you're encouraged to use the same method with someone sitting on the chair next to you and thereby increase the healing energy in the room. There is no training, no waiting, and no doubting, just love. Who is to say that one method is better than another? Maybe we would be able to judge between different healers if we were enlightened, but until then a good means of sorting the wheat from the chaff is to check the motivation and results. And for each one of you, it depends on what 'turns you on'. I do think Lency's form of healing is a more feminine energy, which is why it does seem very effective at reaching into men who 'just cannot express their emotions' and allowing them to release blocks. But that is my perception and someone else might immediately contradict me.

The healing which Chuck Spezzano (her husband) uses is , he says, far less powerful than his wife's, but it has certainly healed a great number of people. He is an American Italian who wears bright shirts and uses 'Psychology of Vision' as his tool. For him, the way to reach in and find the root cause of any problem is the gift of the gab, dosed with a mass of insight and inspiration. For analytical minds like my own, I find this method most helpful. Some people need to talk, or need to keep their finger on the pulse, in order to understand. If they don't hear it, or can't explain it, they don't trust it. For these, silent healing is too simple!

Others, too shy for the verbal or touchy variety of healing, might prefer to use written methods. When in the mid-eighties Louise Hay's book 'You Can Heal Your life' was all the rage, somebody British produced a copycat book, but enclosed a mirror on the inside front cover. It was felt that the British would just not be able to look in the bathroom mirror and sing out aloud, "*I love and approve of myself.*" However, while commuting to London on the tube train, one could discreetly look at the inside cover and silently mouth the words whilst retaining some decent British self-composure and stiff upper-lip-ness.

Might I divert for a moment to the time when I first studied Reiki and was one of those very same commuters? So keen was I on using the Reiki hand positions and so lacking in the normal British reserve that I closed my eyes on the busy tube and started placing my hands on my heart. A few seconds later I was rudely awakened by a sharp tap on the arm and a female asking loudly "Are you all right, or are you having a heart attack?" Sh happened to be a female surgeon.... Back to the necessity o balance in all things.

So, yes, some people need to heal by writing out their feeling in the form of a dialogue, or writing a letter to a dead relative t clear up unfinished business. They need to do it by themselves i their own way, with the healer simply pointing to the metho which is most helpful for them. It can work just as effectively.

Nevertheless caution is advisable. I once heard the sorry tale o a large, well-known festival where 'healing water' was on sale. I sold very well at a dollar a glass. What people didn't know wa that the merchant was filling up his bottles at the taps (faucets in the local public lavatory. There is a fine balance betwee gullibility and open-hearted faith.

So if you have been fortunate enough to find a type of healin that suits you, develop it. Stick with it if you wish, or learn othe forms as well. All forms of healing have value for someone, an it may be that eventually you develop your own. I use a numbe of different forms of healing to suit the moment and the patien

I was once told of a student who went to see her belove spiritual teacher, bringing with her loads of questions. It was once-every-two-year occasion and she believed she was usin this very precious time in the best possible fashion. She had als arranged an appointment for her husband. She was horrified t learn that her husband had spent the allotted twenty minutes jus laughing and saying nothing.

Everyone has his or her own way! It is said that we're all mad up of earth, air, fire, water and space, and so it seems mos natural that we should be drawn to different types of healing according to our natural tendencies. Why should all of us have t try to squeeze into the same shoe?

If it is truth, it comes from the one Source. I mean by that, that love is; love is love. You can disguise it in all sorts of ways, but at the root, love is the one thing we all care about, the one thing we all want, and the one thing from which we often shy away. But in all my years of training I have never met anyone who doesn't believe in love. Even the most downtrodden, cynical, pained person knows that if they see a child about to be run over in the street, their first instinct would be to run after them and save them. Even if after the first impulse they decide it's too dangerous or they might get their clothes dirty or be late for work... The fact is everyone has, at root, a good heart. If someone has the intention of tapping into their good heart, they cannot go wrong. The difference is that some might play the piano with one finger and some might become concert pianists. Some just heal their child when they fall over, and others make it their life's journey to heal all sentient beings. The healing still comes from that one Source.

Chapter Eight
Healing, Not Curing

Some people may still confuse healing with curing. The use of healing is spreading to such a degree that this misunderstanding is being cleared up, but there are still many people who are attracted to healing but who shy away because of 'the curing angle'. It is for this very reason, that healing is not curing, that the local hospital will employ all types of alternative therapists but not healers. Yet a 'Which' survey (November '95) revealed that 75% of respondents said they felt much better as a result (of healing) – far more than for any other form of therapy. Over half said that their condition had greatly improved – again a higher proportion than for any of the other therapies. In April '98, an article in the Journal of the Royal Society of Medicine stated: "A body of sound research has now been accumulated which for many supports the reality of healing beyond reasonable doubt...." Healing is increasingly seen as a technique which can provide benefits to patients with a wide range of ailments while being relatively inexpensive and without the side-effects which may arise from treatments provided by modern medicine. Daniel Benor, an indefatigable researcher into healing, writes: "There is more research evidence to support the efficacy of healing than there is for any other therapy with the exception of psycho-neuro immunology." He also adds, "if healing were a drug one could market, it would long ago have been on the shelves."[1]

[1] Daniel Benor, *Healing Research,* Volume 1

So why are people so scared and reticent? It may be cynicis[m]
but I believe it is because healing is not a 'profession' li[ke]
acupuncture and osteopathy. Have you noticed how these tw[o]
trades have become more orthodox than orthodox? No doubt t[he]
blame lies with some healing practitioners as well. There are lo[ts]
of airy-fairy people who have done disservice to our trade, but [we]
should not be under-estimated for that reason. It is impossible [to]
test people on the contents of the previous chapters and so it [is]
impossible for healing to really be professional. Healing li[es]
beyond the suits and labels.

It might also serve to provide a simple definition. I offer thi[s:]
healing means a return to wholeness. Let me give you a fe[w]
thoughts:

- In German, when you are ill, you are asked: "Was ist los[?"]
  meaning, "What is missing?"

- On one occasion Jesus cured with the words: "Get up, thy si[ns]
  are forgiven."

- If you cut your finger (not too badly, of course), it heals itse[lf.]

The current chairman of the British National Federation [of]
Spiritual Healers is a doctor as well as a healer. His dream is th[at]
every doctor and nurse in the country will incorporate heali[ng]
into their work... It is a big dream and one which could becom[e]
reality if people's misunderstandings and fears dissipate.

So why does healing not mean curing? Because, if I treat a si[ck]
person and they are dying, we both know that they are not goi[ng]
to be cured. It is immoral to promise that to anyone. Everyone h[as]
a set life span and nobody can go against that. Yet many dyi[ng]
patients have died healed. This is not a contradiction. Let m[e]
explain by example.

One very sad case was of a young mother who rang me fro[m]
her hospital bed. My first question to her was, "Do you want [to]
live?" To *her* astonishment, her reply was, "No." This was t[he]

beginning of an intense search and much inner development. By the time she came close to passing on, she told me that she did now want to live. The difference was that she had been on such a journey of self-discovery that she now *knew* that she *would* 'live' after her physical death. The toughest way to learn, but she learnt it.

The other case I would like to write about concerns the most tragic person I have treated. She was also my greatest teacher. Let's call her D. She was 32 with two young children and had absolutely no faith whatsoever. She had had cancer in her early twenties, got better, married, had two children and then developed cancer of the spine. This spread rapidly. She went through unbearable suffering. As she was losing her life, I gave birth to my third child. She, a Taurus who liked her possessions, gave me all her youngest son's clothes.

She so wanted to believe in something. She so wanted her father to be 'on the other side' for her. I had been seeing her on and off for two years and increased my visits as she got weaker and weaker. She saw others and talked to priests and to everyone who might help her find her path. She used to ask me what happened when you die. She told me how it had been like a dream when she sat with the consultant and he had told her she only had weeks to live and there was nothing she could do. She cried with me when a consultant shoved me out of the way to tell her 'she *must* feel better' because he had performed yet another fancy operation on her which had no effect whatsoever. She listened to the tapes I gave her and tried to meditate. All to no avail. She was scared. She didn't want to let go. It grieves me to remember the time when I went to see her at home and she could no longer walk. Her husband, already working full-time and caring for the two children, looked absolutely exhausted as he reached into the fridge to start cooking supper. So little back-up to help them. Hospices are not hotels, she was told. She used to lie at home all day on her own, too weak to move and without anyone to see her. One day when I visited, a Japanese student was

looking through the mail-slot in her front door. He had bee
ringing the doorbell again and again, and she was trying to stan
up on crutches (which was excruciatingly painful for her) to g
to him. He couldn't understand her, and she couldn't understan
him. It turned out that he was looking for another house and ha
the wrong house number...

She watched as she became 'dispensable' and in bitter pain sh
told me she had understood that her husband could cope withou
her, but agonised that even her children could too. She made
through her last Christmas, buying them the most beautiful hug
Christmas stockings and one of those books from Fathe
Christmas addressed to the child.

The Aromatherapy essence 'Rose' was the only thing whic
lifted her spirits. She also told me she had never heard 'sublim
music. So I tried to make her a tape of such music. Not easy. An
suggestions gratefully received. She listened to it in the hospic
when she was unconscious, but I knew she heard it. Still sh
searched. I involved those greater than myself and knew the
were praying for her. And finally she died. She happened to di
when the one hospice nurse was present who could 'lead h
through it'. The nurse told me it worked.

At her funeral (which was packed) the vicar told us all that he
last words on the tape she had been making for her children were

'I can help so many people'.

I honestly believe that she transcended her suffering and trul
came to understand the meaning of compassion.

It is said not to be good to talk about personal experiences, bu
I would like to share one with you, hoping that it will be c
benefit to those of you who doubt, or are terrified of death. I ha
always known with an inner profound faith that consciousne
didn't end at death and had of course 'read all about it', but I ha
not had a near-death experience like so many other people an
so could not say, 'I know'. Several weeks after D's death, I wa

treating a patient called Gill who believed in angels. Not for me to agree or disagree.

On that particular day, I felt the presence of D. I do know how batty you may think I am, but I have no reason to lie. She flew by me over my left shoulder, much smaller in my vision than in life,. She smiled a beaming glowing smile, waved her wand and zoomed onwards. I could tell she was so happy: *she was helping others.*

That was it. I am so grateful for that glimpse. It was proof. She was healed, not cured.

The curious thing is her husband remarried quite shortly afterwards and is very happy with a third child. Given our limited perception, all our pain comes from our attachment to seeing something as it isn't. Or, as the saying goes, man proposes, God disposes. Things are not as they seem nor as we wish them to be, but everything is perfect as it is. We just can't see it.

Death is such a scary topic for people. Why? It's the one thing we can be sure will happen. A few years back I went on a wonderful course with Christine Longaker whose book, 'Facing Death and Finding Hope', is excellent. I stayed with some friends of mine in London who were giving one of those dinner parties. When the conversation turned to my reason for being in London, and they were told, the subject changed rapidly. At the end, as one of the ladies left, she whispered to me, "Great work, but not for now."

So when is it for? When we've dropped dead from a heart attack?

My father is 78 and we regularly talk about his death. He's given all his children a copy of his will. All potential acrimony arises now before he dies. For example, he knows I am irritated because he wants his 'sons' to scatter his ashes, not his daughter. He also knows I will do prayers for him and have one of my teachers do more effective ones. We cry together. All this makes

more precious the time that we have alive now. We still argue an
get crotchety, but the important issues are dealt with.
recommend it. It is all part of healing, be it for others c
ourselves.

Having understood the difference between healing and curing
it may be useful to see how the healer can help when a dyin
patient is to be treated. If you're called upon, it's often becaus
the nurses or doctors or friends or families are not 'filling th
gap'. It could also be because they want you to perform a miracl
They need to be disabused of that idea. So how can you b
useful? You can't be if you're frightened. You can't be if you'r
full of yourself. I can only make a few suggestions. These are nc
the only ones, but I hope will help a little.

I will mention once again that I always spend a few minute
meditating before entering the hospital or home. Life is so intens
when you are losing it, and the healer has to be clear.

1 Be calm

2 Be ready to listen

3 Don't talk about the weather. There are umpteen others doin
   that

4 Don't stay long

5 Talk about the things that others are scared of talking about

6 If asked, and if you feel able, explain how you understand th
   'afterlife'

7 Only speak the truth. Patients are ultra-sensitive and pick u
   on the gaps.

8 Do the practice of exchange, the whole time you are there, an
   before and afterwards

9 Hold their hands and place your concentration on that. Usin
   all the hand positions can impede concentration, and possibl

increase pain. Using the hand positions is also difficult if they are lying in bed. But if it is easy, I love to place my hands over the head as well.

10 If the person is very close to death, don't even hold their hands. Something very useful which I recently learned is that consciousness ejects out of the crown of the head. It is therefore most important not to bring the person's focus back into the body. If you can stroke the crown of their head, that would be the most effective thing you can do for them.

11 Know your place. The medical fraternity, and often the other relatives, are too tied up doing their own thing. You are there for the patient. Do what you can and leave. Don't get fussily involved.

12 Don't be silent out of fear or because you can't think of the 'proper' thing to say. I've often heard of people's frustrations because relatives sit around without speaking, or only speak about trite matters. It's like not looking at somebody in a wheelchair, and speaking only to the person who is pushing them. Just because a person is dying does not mean they've gone gaga or are without the need to express themselves. Be sensitive.

13 Know that when the person does breathe their last, it is not all over. Keep on sending them light or doing the practice of exchange for weeks. It will carry on helping them and you. In the Tibetan tradition it is recommended that you do not cry. I have not managed to achieve this at all, but it is said to draw the dead person's consciousness back instead of allowing it to move on. If one could only truly realise that grief is only one's own selfish grief and not really the dying/dead person's, it could help stave off some of the emotion. A tricky one.... Perhaps it's 'stiff upper lip' at its best: Princess Diana did not cry at her father's funeral...

There is so much more to say on this subject, but I hope these few pointers are helpful. If you know them already and have other useful suggestions, please send them to me.

Chapter Nine
Questions and Answers

I hope the following will answer some of the questions you may still have. Some of them are tricky ones to which I can offer but a limited view from my personal experience. I hope the answers are of some help.

How often should I give healing?

Always a difficult one to answer. If laying on hands in a perfect setting, I always recommend seeing patients three times with a week's gap in between each time. Of all patients, 99% will feel an effect after the first treatment, but some need three before they begin to 'unwind' on a more long-term basis. After that I leave it up to the patient. Their decision can be part of their treatment. Otherwise money or attachment can come into either side of the equation. Sometimes people are a little insecure and guidance can be helpful, but I do not think you need to prescribe long, obligatory courses of treatment.

If you have a 'difficult' case (such as a referral where the patient has tried many other courses of treatment without success) and there are no money problems, longer courses of treatment will undoubtedly be advisable to begin to shift blocks.

If some one has cancer or some disease where things are not looking good, the healing is up to them as well as you. It is likely

to be ongoing treatment. For those who can afford it, the mor
treatments the better, and you can charge less because of th
frequency. I've always had the rule that I don't charge if I vis
patients in hospital. It doesn't feel right. But equally, with tim
being as precious as it is, it does not work if I take on a patien
and then cannot be there for others because that patient is takin
all my time. *You* need to be the judge in each case, and you nee
to keep a sense of balance. So many healers (including me!) go
big heads and can think we are needed: remember we ar
dispensable as well. I repeat Manning's words: "Are you ther
because you've got love to give, or because you need love?"

Equally, you can always do absent healing and there is no tim
limit to that. Nor do you need to charge...

Should I charge money or not?

This question has taken me years to sort out. My persona
conclusion is this. If you don't charge, people don't necessaril
respect the work you do. So many people go and see their Britis
GPs on the National Health because they don't have to pay.
they had to, they either wouldn't bother or they would be mor
willing to listen to and act upon the GPs' advice. Veering ont
another subject, have you noticed how doctors are becomin
priests as well?

I have been in the fortunate position of receiving doctor
referrals, but I can guarantee that those patients will not have th
same desire to heal as those who are paying. They're coming fror
different positions. One still needs 'big daddy', the other doesn'
One still needs to be 'out of balance', the other wants to fee
whole. This isn't to say that the former will not improve, bu
perhaps they need more guidance. And there are alway
exceptions to that rule.

It also boils down to your own balance. If you have a famil
to feed and you are giving out free healing all the time, are yo

acting from a position of compassion or sacrifice? A well-off spiritualist friend of mine used to charge a modest fee. She had decided that if she didn't, she would be hindering the people who needed to earn money by healing from doing so. Of course, one is not really earning money from healing. How can one earn money for love? One is charging for the time spent with the patient and the time spent on 'training'. What goes out, comes back. What comes in, goes out. If you can't feed yourself, how can you feed others? You need to find the right flow.

As for charging friends, that's your choice as well. How does *your* desire to impose *your* belief that you can help them weigh against their desire to receive healing? It is usually only friends who don't turn up or who take the treatment for granted. If that is going to upset you, perhaps it is better to do the practice of exchange once again. Then you will *both* feel better, without any issues arising.

I grew up with my father being asked at every single social occasion to look at someone's ingrown toenail or the pimple on their abdomen. He would always oblige, but at what cost to the other guests and squirmy people present? I often put my hands on people on social occasions, because the opportunity presents itself, but I forget how strange it may seem to others. It can make them feel uncomfortable. They can also start making judgements, such as you're doing it because "you've had a glass of wine," or because "you've just been yelling at your wife/husband." One must ask what is best for the recipient? Each occasion merits a different response.

If you have been on a week's retreat or workshop, you may have been fortunate enough to have experienced how the negativity of your daily life slips away. By day three or four, the natural love kicks in. By day five or six, everyone is offering everyone else some kind of therapy. Everyone is hugging, thinking kind thoughts, and giving healing, Reiki, massage or x, y, z. In other words, in the right environment, all the relative judgements and opinions, as well as money, become obsolete Thank goodness! The world could of course become the extension of that environment...!

Should we stop taking orthodox medicine?

I am ultra-orthodox on this subject. I see no problem with people continuing their course of orthodox medicine while they are receiving healing. Of course, I believe pills are oversubscribed and over-used and often used to ill effect, but I do not believe in throwing out the baby with the bath water. I know a doctor who set up a hospital to treat people with mental problems without using drugs of any kind. Very sadly indeed, it did not work. That is not to say that if you treat someone on a long-term basis in conjunction with a doctor, that they would not be able to cut down on their tablets. Yet this does need the co-operation of the medical fraternity.

It is of course now well-known that antibiotics are often proving ineffective, and yet they too still play a life-saving role. When my daughter was six months old and contracted periorbital cellulitis, I was the first to let her have a course of antibiotics in spite of the fact that I was using other methods of healing at the same time. *Antibiotics may have saved her life and not using them may have killed her.*

At a Doctor Healer Network meeting a few months later, I met a Russian doctor who was also a healer. She was working in Harley street and was troubled because all her patients came to see her because of her renown as a healer. They refused to take antibiotics even when, as a doctor, she would explain that the antibiotics would produce the healing they wanted. She was herself becoming confused as to whether she should insist. When I quoted the extreme example of my daughter's case, her doubts vanished and common sense returned. Another case where faith needs to be combined with skilful means...

Why doesn't healing always work?

Aah! It does always work even if it doesn't. Does that sound like R.D. Laing? (famous in the sixties for his book, 'Knots'). As discussed already, you may not see a cure, but at some level it will do its work. At worst, the person will feel calmer. At best, the person will be healed. In between those two extremes there lies a lot of ground. Many people will come with a sore toe. They may still leave with a sore toe, but if they feel more peaceful about it, their pain is relieved.

I always love a story told by Ram Dass about his teacher. His teacher was riddled with cancer of the stomach and one of his disciples turned to him and asked: "Doesn't it hurt?" The teacher replied, whilst roaring with laughter: "It feels like a million bees are stinging me at once." The point was that the pain didn't distract him. He was still laughing. Pain is so much worse when we are attached to it. Another student went to see their teacher and asked: "And what about my arthritis?" The teacher replied: "Let's go and see all the other arthritises." The student was deeply hurt, but it was only his ego that was hurt. He learned that the way out of pain was to concentrate on others. If the patient learns compassion, they learn to heal themselves. That's the irony. Healing is ultimately selfish: through others, we learn to heal ourselves. That may not be our motivation, but the two go hand in hand.

And yes, cures do happen. The miracle and the danger zone are one. Matthew Manning now has proof that he has killed off cancer cells. He also has patients who should be dead but who are full of life, many years on. Wonderful! Miracles do occur. But we do need to distinguish. I am not speaking of the type of so-called healing where, because of heightened group energy, people get out of their wheelchairs only to fall down again a few hours later, but of the real, long-lasting miracles. I have no doubt that they occur because the patient was in the right place at the right time with the right person. It was their karma that the miracle should

occur. They had learned what they needed to, and no long
needed the 'disease'.

For many years I believed that if someone had enough fait
those miracles would occur. So when I became ill, I expected
miracle because I had so much faith. What a precious lesson!
doesn't work that way. Healer, heal thyself! I had to learn tha
sometimes karma needs to wear off. I can speed up the process c
healing through prayer and practice, but I cannot negate
through faith alone, and neither can God or Buddha or Alla!
How disappointing! But that explains why the world is as it i
Otherwise God, Buddha or Allah could simply will us all to b
permanently free from suffering.

Taking the thought a step further (and for the sake of thos
readers who are going through living hell, I do not wish to b
flippant about this), would you want to be in permanent heaven
I recall there was a book about just that: people had everythin
they wanted all the time and they hated it! As Chuck Spezzan
puts it: "If we were on a cloud now, looking down and choosin
our life, would we choose a life lying on a beach in Bermuda c
our life as we have it now?" If we're really honest, I think w
would choose what we have, warts and all. So successful healin
can also mean the realisation that our suffering is our learnin
path. Not that we need to stay in it. Not that we cannot trai
ourselves to get out of it. Simply that through compassion we ca
sublimate it. If somebody learns to meditate and do the practic
of exchange, healing takes place within, and maybe later it wi
take place at a physical level. So true healing lies within.

Sometimes we need to learn patience. Doctors who have spen
their lives in medicine will tell you that, whereas in the pas
people did not expect immediate results, today they want to b
cured *right now, immediately.* They expect the pill they're give
to have a complete effect straight away. That doesn't work eithe
Sure, you can take pills to cover up the pain, but that's lik
papering over the cracks in a wall. You still need to fill in th

holes. That's why having flu can really be of benefit. It really can mean a clearing out process for somebody who would otherwise never switch off. Only when they can no longer stand up and look at their paperwork or laptop, can they let the body and mind do what *they* need to do. For once they let go of control! So flu can be the healer. The laying-on of hands may relieve the symptoms or may make matters worse; whatever is needed will occur.

How many times has my ego wanted a particular result! I've stopped that now. I let the healing do what it will. It's always a surprise. A 'miracle' will happen when I least expect it, and nothing when I most want it to. 'I' have nothing to do with it, except to be bossy and encourage people to do their homework: meditation, mind training, you know the form by now...

How long does a session need to be?

This varies as well. You will get to sense it with experience. As a guide, look for twenty minutes to talk, twenty minutes to do a visualisation or psychological process and twenty minutes for healing. Most often, twenty minutes of hands-on is sufficient. Sometimes forty minutes is wonderful, and that can feel like a real treat. Sometimes ten minutes is sufficient. Some people can only take so much.

I've noticed that the most powerful healing is when time stops. What seems to me like hours will seem to the patient like a second, and vice-versa. Strange but true. The true healing takes place out of time.

When do I offer healing?

When you're asked, and at no other time. You can always do the practice of exchange 'without permission', but hands-on healing needs the other's participation.

Do you need the patient to believe?

Absolutely not. Matthew Manning's book, *No Faith Required,* is an excellent title. He has proved that cancer cells in test tubes respond to healing. Test tube cancer cells don't have faith. That is not to decry faith, just to say that it is not vital.

Why do people feel such heat in the healer's hands?

No idea. Tests have shown the temperature does not change. Maybe the power of thought? Analogously, electrics often go wrong when psychics who are out of balance are around ...

What about absent healing?

If you do the practice of exchange, you are practising absent healing. If you wish to be more formal, you can do it during your meditation practice and use a photo of the person or people concerned. It is best to do it over and over again.

How long before you can set up practice?

That is for you to judge. When you have the confidence, and know that you are coming from the heart.

How do I know I am 'doing it right'?

You don't. People will come and, if you're helping, they'll keep on coming. If you're not, they won't. Don't expect hordes. Healing is not a money-spinner unless you're exceptional. It comes and goes, as you need it for your learning. Keep the motivation as pure as you can.

People seem to get better. Is that me?

No, it's not you. It might be the healing. There are always so many factors. I like to think that it is the patients themselves who have allowed the block to dissolve. That might be through a combination of orthodox medicine, their positive determination and the visit to see you. Who knows? Not you or I, unless we're enlightened.

How long was your training?

Lifelong (or many lifetimes long), and it's only just begun.

May you enjoy your journey as much as I have enjoyed mine. May you benefit as many people as possible. May love be with you!

　Don't worry, be happy.

References and Recommended Reading

Books Referenced in the Text

Benor, Daniel. *Healing Research, vol. 1*, revised edition. Vision Publications, Southfield, MI 2000.

Chodron, Pema. *Start Where You Are*. Shambhala, Boston 1994.

Chopra, Deepak. *Perfect Weight*. Harmony Books, 1994.

Hay, Louise. *You Can Heal Your Life*. Eden Grove Editions, Santa Monica, CA 1984.

Journal of the Royal Society of Medicine, Volume 91, April 1998, pp. 183-188.

Laing, R.D. *Knots*. Pantheon Books, NY 1970.

Manning, Matthew. *A Foot in the Stars*. Element, Shaftesbury, Dorset, UK 1999.

Sheldrake, Rupert. *The Rebirth of Nature*. Bantam, NY 1991.

Spezzano, Chuck. *If It Hurts, It Isn't Love*. Hodder and Stoughton, London 1999.

TichNatHan. *Breathe, You Are Alive*. TBerkeley, CA 1998.

BOOKS RECOMMENDED FOR FURTHER READING

Brown, Craig. *Optimum Healing*. Rider, London 1999.

Kingston, Karen. *Creating Sacred Space with Feng-Shui*. Piatkus, London 1996.

Longaker, Christine. *Facing Death and Finding Hope*. Random House, UK 1997.

Manning, Matthew. *No Faith Required*. Eikstein Publications, Norway 1995.

Sogyal Rinpoche. *The Tibetan Book of Living and Dying*. Harper, San Francisco 1992.

Spezzano, Lency. *Make Way for Love*. Psychology of Vision Press, 1995.

His Holiness the Dalai Lama – any book you pick, and he should be at the top of the list.

Chodron, Pema – ditto

Chopra, Deepak – ditto

Kabat-Zinn, John – ditto

Levine, Stephen – ditto

Linn, Denise – ditto

Spezzano, Chuck – ditto

Weil, Andrew – ditto

The above are not in order of preference and represent but a few.